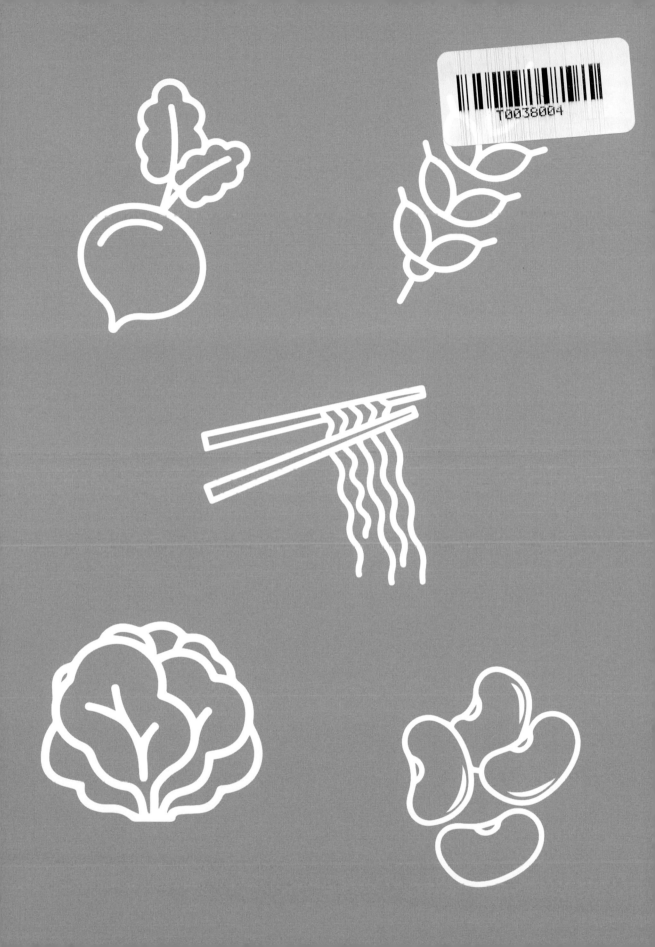

THE
5-MINUTE
Noodle Salad
LUNCHBOX

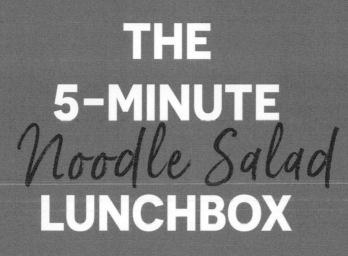

THE 5-MINUTE NOODLE SALAD LUNCHBOX

HAPPY, HEALTHY & SPEEDY
SALADS TO MAKE
IN MINUTES

ALEXANDER HART

Smith
Street
Books

CONTENTS

INTRODUCTION

The packed lunch is often the first thing to fly out the door in the weekday morning routine. Whether you have your hands full wrangling the rest of the household into the car, are racing off to get some pre-work endorphins, or just squeezing in a few extra minutes of shut-eye, toiling over a homemade lunch can easily fall completely off the morning's to-do list. Not least because thinking about what to make every day is exhausting. But it doesn't have to be.

These 52 noodle salad recipes are here to ease the burden of everyone's least favourite midday conundrum: what to eat for lunch. Speedy, healthy, inexpensive and, most importantly, packed with flavour, this book has delicious lunchtime answers for every week of the year.

A long way from the humble sandwich, the noodle salads in this book are colourful, nutritious and filling creations that won't break the bank or send you into a post-lunch slump. Separated into five chapters, explore recipes for Hokkien, Ramen, Rice, Soba and Veggie noodle salads – that can all be whipped up in a swift five minutes!

Each salad is paired with a tasty dressing that can be prepared in advance and kept in an air-tight container in the fridge. Homemade is always best, but in a pinch, you can always reach for store-bought. The point is to make things as easy as possible for yourself.

The salads in this book have been designed to quickly prep before work or study and will maintain all their deliciousness and crunch so long as you keep the dressing separate. We recommend using a fraction of the money you'll save from skipping the takeaway lunch and investing in a lunchbox with a dedicated dressing compartment to avoid being met with a sad soggy salad come noon. Each of the recipes are designed for one, but if you're making lunches for more or if you're particularly smitten with one of the recipes, just double the portions.

Lunchtime shouldn't be a chore, but that doesn't mean it needs to come with a hefty price tag. Curb your costly, and often unhealthy, takeaway habits and use these 52 noodle salad recipes to start your delicious, healthy and budget-friendly lunch routine.

SALAD INGREDIENTS

Here are a few notes on some of the ingredients used in this book, along with tips and tricks to help cut down your prep time even further.

BEANS & LENTILS

Although the recipes in this book call for tinned beans and lentils, as they're a speedy option for adding to salads, you can, of course, soak and cook your own beans and lentils ahead of time and store them in the fridge. One major advantage of this is that you'll avoid the salt and sugar in the brine tinned varieties are stored in.

BEETROOT

Cooked beetroot (beets) are available from the supermarket, usually in jars for baby beetroot and a vacuum-sealed packet for the larger variety. Mix it up and use golden or target beetroot when they're in season.

CHEESE

Good-quality hard cheeses such as parmesan and pecorino can be purchased shaved, grated or shredded, while crumbled feta is available in tubs in the refrigerated section of your supermarket.

COOKED CHICKEN

Shredded cooked chicken is available from your supermarket deli. Alternatively, buy or cook a whole roast chicken, chop or shred the meat yourself and store in an airtight container in the fridge for up to 4 days. Another healthy option (if you have time) is to poach some chicken breasts for use throughout the week.

DRESSINGS

For most of the recipes in this book, the dressing is kept separately so you can dress your salad just before you eat it. You can save yourself some more time in the morning by mixing your dressing the night before and keeping the container in the fridge. You could even prep a whole week's worth in advance.

HARD-BOILED EGGS

Cook a batch ahead of time and keep in the fridge for up to 1 week. To prepare, place your eggs in a saucepan and cover with cold water. Bring to the boil over medium–high heat, then cover, remove from the heat and set aside for 8–11 minutes (depending on how hard you like them). Drain, cool in iced water and peel just before adding to your salad.

HERBS

To save time, chop all of your fresh herbs together.

MINCED GARLIC & GINGER

Available in jars – or tubes (usually sold as 'paste') – from the supermarket, these really are a time-saving wonder. Alternatively, you can make your own: blitz a large quantity of garlic or fresh ginger in a food processor with a little water, salt and a drop of oil. It will keep well in an airtight container in the fridge for up to 2 weeks, or press flat in a zip-lock bag and store in the freezer for up to 2 months.

PRE-CUT VEGETABLES

Supermarkets carry a large range of packaged pre-cut vegetables that keep well in your fridge, which is what we recommend using to keep your prep time to around 5 minutes. Look for spiralised zucchini (courgette) ('zoodles'), pumpkin (winter squash), beetroot (beets) and other vegetables. You'll also find other convenient combination products, such as coleslaw and mixed salad leaves.

TOASTED NUTS & SEEDS

Toast nuts and seeds ahead of time, leave to cool completely and store in an airtight container in your pantry for up to 1 month.

NOODLES

Hokkien noodles

Hokkien noodles – also referred to as lo mein noodles – are a thick, chewy wheat-based egg noodle. They can usually be purchased pre-cooked and oiled. They can be prepared by steeping them in boiling water for a few minutes before draining them under cold water. Otherwise, follow the packet instructions for preparation.

Ramen noodles

Ramen can refer both to the wheat-based noodle or the iconic Japanese noodle soup dish. The noodles themselves can be purchased as a hard noodle block ('instant ramen'), or soft pre-cooked noodles stored in a vacuum-sealed packet. Both sorts are used in the recipes – the instant ramen variety kept uncooked for its crunch. Check the packet instructions, but the pre-cooked variety needs to steep in boiling water for a few minutes before rinsing under cold water and draining.

Rice noodles

We use three different types of rice noodles in the recipes: rice vermicelli noodles; flat rice stick or pad Thai noodles; and wide rice noodles. Each vary in width, with vermicelli being the thinnest and wide rice noodles the fattest. Check the packet instructions, but these varieties should cook in boiling water in 2–3 minutes; otherwise, steep in boiling water for 4–5 minutes. Rinse under cold water and drain.

Soba noodles

Soba are a Japanese-style buckwheat flour noodle that have an earthy, moreish flavour. There are many types on the market – with some swapping out the buckwheat for wheat flour entirely – so find your favourite. The noodles can also be purchased in dried and pre-cooked forms, so prepare them according to the packet instructions.

Veggie noodles

At one stage, there were only zucchini (courgette) 'zoodles' – but now there are so many more options for creating vegetable-based 'noodles'. Arm yourself with a good-quality spiraliser and almost any hard vegetable can be spiralised into healthy noodles!

NOTES ON THE RECIPES

While the recipes are designed to be simple and quick to prepare, do ensure you read through the entire recipe before starting.

NOTES ON QUANTITIES

We find you rarely need exact quantities when putting together a salad, so we've used 'handfuls of' in many cases, making ingredients quick to throw in. Feel free to adjust the quantities to make use of what you might already have in your fridge.

All tablespoons are 15 ml / 3 teaspoons.

HOKKIEN NOODLES

SATAY CHICKEN NOODLE SALAD

This noodle salad offers up a delicious combination of flavours – and is colourful, too! To cut down further on the preparation time, use a good-quality store-bought satay dressing that is low in sugar.

180 g (6½ oz) thin hokkien noodles, prepared as per packet instructions

100 g (3½ oz) shredded cooked chicken

1 small spring onion (scallion), finely sliced

½ short cucumber, finely sliced

¼ red bell pepper (capsicum), finely sliced

2 tablespoons peanuts, chopped

small handful of coriander (cilantro) leaves

pinch of dried chilli flakes

SATAY DRESSING

3 tablespoons peanut butter

1½ tablespoons rice vinegar

juice of ½ lime

1 teaspoon kecap manis (sweet soy sauce)

1 teaspoon sriracha sauce

1 Toss all the salad ingredients together, then tip into your lunchbox.

2 Combine the dressing ingredients in a small jar or container with a tight-fitting lid; you may need to add a little water.

3 Pour the dressing over the salad just before serving and toss well.

CRUNCHY NOODLE SALAD WITH CASHEWS

Celery, cucumber, snow peas and cashews add all the crunch in this moreish vegetarian noodle salad. Feel free to add or substitute other crunchy vegetables such as radishes, sugar snap peas or bell pepper (capsicum) – and swap out the cashews for roasted almonds, pecans or walnuts.

180 g (6½ oz) hokkien noodles, prepared as per packet instructions

1 celery stalk, finely sliced

½ short cucumber, finely sliced

50 g (1¾ oz) snow peas (mangetout), finely sliced

handful of roasted cashews

2 teaspoons toasted sesame seeds

TAHINI GINGER DRESSING

2 tablespoons tahini

4 teaspoons rice vinegar

4 teaspoons kecap manis (sweet soy sauce)

1 teaspoon minced ginger

1 Toss all the salad ingredients together, then tip into your lunchbox.

2 Combine the dressing ingredients in a small jar or container with a tight-fitting lid; you may need to add a little water.

3 Pour the dressing over the salad just before serving and toss well.

HOKKIEN NOODLES WITH TUNA & CHILLI OIL

Ponzu is a classic Japanese condiment with a citrus-like taste, giving this salad a deliciously tart–tangy flavour. Seek out good-quality tinned tuna with good texture – it can really lift this recipe.

180 g (6½ oz) hokkien noodles, prepared as per packet instructions

95 g (3¼ oz) tin tuna in chilli oil (including the oil from the tin)

6 cherry tomatoes, halved

¼ red bell pepper (capsicum), finely sliced

handful of mixed salad greens

fresh sliced chilli, to taste

PONZU DRESSING

1 tablespoon ponzu

2 teaspoons rice vinegar

1½ teaspoons sesame oil

1 Toss the salad ingredients together, then tip into your lunchbox.

2 Combine the dressing ingredients in a small jar or container with a tight-fitting lid.

3 Pour the dressing over the salad just before serving and toss well.

CHORIZO, CHICKPEA & ROASTED PEPPER NOODLE SALAD

Chorizo is a Spanish-style cured pork sausage that comes in many forms – including fresh and cured varieties. Fresh chorizo needs to be sliced and fried for a few minutes before use, while cured varieties require no cooking. Either can be used in this recipe.

◇◇◇◇◇◇◇◇◇◇

180 g (6½ oz) thin hokkien noodles, prepared as per packet instructions

1 roasted red bell pepper (capsicum), finely sliced

50 g (1¾ oz) dried or smoked chorizo, finely sliced

85 g (½ cup) tinned chickpeas, rinsed and drained

⅛ small red onion, finely sliced

handful of cherry tomatoes, halved

handful of rocket (arugula) leaves

SHERRY VINAIGRETTE

1 tablespoon extra virgin olive oil

2 teaspoons sherry vinegar

1 teaspoon dijon mustard

1 teaspoon agave syrup, honey or maple syrup

salt and pepper, to taste

 Toss all the salad ingredients together, then tip into your lunchbox.

 Combine the dressing ingredients in a small jar or container with a tight-fitting lid.

 Pour the dressing over the salad just before serving and toss well.

CHICKEN & PINEAPPLE NOODLES WITH GOCHUJANG

Gochujang is a Korean red chilli paste that can be variously spicy, savoury and sweet, depending on the brand. It adds a complex, deliciously deep flavour and perfectly counterpoints the sweetness of the pineapple in this dish. You'll find it in most supermarkets and Asian grocers.

180 g (6½ oz) hokkien noodles, prepared as per packet instructions

100 g (3½ oz) shredded cooked chicken

60 g (⅓ cup) chopped pineapple

1 spring onion (scallion), finely sliced

2 teaspoons toasted black sesame seeds

GOCHUJANG DRESSING

1 tablespoon gochujang paste

1 teaspoon kecap manis (sweet soy sauce)

1 teaspoon rice vinegar

1 teaspoon soy sauce

1 teaspoon toasted sesame oil

½ teaspoon water

1 Toss the salad ingredients together, then tip into your lunchbox.

2 Combine the dressing ingredients in a small jar or container with a tight-fitting lid.

3 Pour the dressing over the salad just before serving and toss well.

CAPRESE & PROSCIUTTO NOODLE SALAD

The caprese salad is a classic Italian dish of tomatoes, fresh mozzarella and basil leaves – the three colours of the Italian flag. This recipe includes those ingredients, alongside noodles and prosciutto, to create a more substantial lunch!

180 g (6½ oz) hokkien noodles, prepared as per packet instructions

2–3 slices prosciutto, torn

handful of heirloom cherry tomatoes, halved

handful of basil leaves

½ fresh mozzarella ball, torn

1 tablespoon toasted pine nuts

SUN-DRIED TOMATO & CHILLI VINAIGRETTE

4 teaspoons extra virgin olive oil

1 tablespoon aged balsamic vinegar

1 tablespoon diced sun-dried tomato

pinch of dried chilli flakes

1 Toss all the salad ingredients together, then tip into your lunchbox.

2 Combine the dressing ingredients in a small jar or container with a tight-fitting lid.

3 Pour the dressing over the salad just before serving and toss well.

NOODLES WITH ROASTED PUMPKIN, LENTILS & BABY SPINACH

This is a great salad option to prepare the day after you've cooked a roast dinner! If you don't have almond butter to hand, try using tahini or even a good-quality peanut butter instead.

180 g (6½ oz) hokkien noodles, prepared as per packet instructions

150 g (5½ oz) left-over roasted pumpkin (winter squash), diced

100 g (3½ oz) drained tinned lentils

handful of baby spinach leaves

handful of toasted almonds, chopped

salt and pepper, to taste

ALMOND MISO DRESSING

2 tablespoons almond butter

2 tablespoons orange juice

1 teaspoon white (shiro) miso paste

1 teaspoon rice vinegar

½ teaspoon maple syrup, honey or agave syrup

1. Toss all the salad ingredients together, then tip into your lunchbox.

2. Combine the dressing ingredients in a small jar or container with a tight-fitting lid; you may need to add a little water.

3. Pour the dressing over the salad just before serving and toss well.

BEEF & BROCCOLINI CASHEW NOODLE SALAD

These days you can buy slices of roast beef from good-quality delicatessens or butchers to toss through this deliciously hearty salad. Simply omit the bird's eye chilli or choose a milder long red chilli if you prefer less spice.

180 g (6½ oz) hokkien noodles, prepared as per packet instructions

100 g (3½ oz) sliced roast beef, cut into strips

3 broccolini stems, cut into 5 cm (2 in) pieces, blanched

⅛ small red onion, finely sliced

1 red bird's eye chilli, sliced

handful of roasted cashews

SESAME, SOY & GINGER DRESSING

2 teaspoons sesame oil

2 teaspoons soy sauce

2 teaspoons rice vinegar

2 teaspoons honey

¼ teaspoon minced garlic

¼ teaspoon minced ginger

1 Toss the salad ingredients together, then tip into your lunchbox.

2 Combine the dressing ingredients in a small jar or container with a tight-fitting lid.

3 Pour the dressing over the salad just before serving and toss well.

NOODLES WITH TEMPEH & MIXED VEGETABLES

Tempeh, a deliciously nutritious ingredient that originates from Indonesia, is created from fermented soybeans. There are many different types of tempeh available, but for the largest range, head to health food stores or specialty Asian grocers.

2 teaspoons olive oil or vegetable oil

100 g (3½ oz) pre-marinated honey soy tempeh, diced

180 g (6½ oz) hokkien noodles, prepared as per packet instructions

100 g (1 cup) mixed frozen vegetables (corn, green beans, carrot, broccoli), blanched

handful of coriander (cilantro) leaves

2 teaspoons toasted sesame seeds

HONEY, PONZU & GINGER DRESSING

2–3 teaspoons honey

2 teaspoons ponzu sauce

2 teaspoons sesame oil

1 teaspoon rice vinegar

1 teaspoon minced ginger

1 Add the oil to a wok and place over medium–high heat. Add the tempeh and cook for 3–4 minutes, until crisp. Remove from the heat and allow to cool.

2 Toss all the salad ingredients together, then tip into your lunchbox.

3 Combine the dressing ingredients in a small jar or container with a tight-fitting lid.

4 Pour the dressing over the salad just before serving and toss well.

CREAMY TURMERIC NOODLES WITH CHICKEN, HERBS & LIME

The turmeric in the dressing adds a lovely yellow hue to this tasty salad. If you're not a fan of coriander, simply omit it from the dish or replace it with parsley – and if you can't get hold of Vietnamese mint, use regular mint instead.

◇◇◇◇◇◇◇◇◇◇

180 g (6½ oz) hokkien noodles, prepared as per packet instructions

100 g (3½ oz) shredded cooked chicken

1 small spring onion (scallion), finely sliced

small handful of coriander (cilantro) leaves

small handful of Vietnamese mint leaves

handful of toasted flaked almonds

2 lime wedges

CREAMY TURMERIC DRESSING

2 tablespoons tahini

2 tablespoons water

1 tablespoon lime juice

1–1½ teaspoons agave syrup, honey or maple syrup

1 teaspoon rice vinegar

¼ teaspoon ground turmeric

1 Place the dressing ingredients in a bowl and whisk to combine. Add the noodles and toss until well coated in the dressing. Add the remaining ingredients, except the lime wedges, and toss again.

2 Tip the noodles into your lunchbox and add the lime wedges.

3 Squeeze the lime over just before serving.

RAMEN NOODLES

MISO MUSHROOM RAMEN NOODLE SALAD

Don't let the lengthy ingredient list put you off whipping up this noodle salad – it's very straightforward, with readily available ingredients! Shiitake mushrooms are native to Japan and China and have a distinctly savoury, almost meaty, flavour.

1 tablespoon sesame oil

1 tablespoon olive oil

100 g (3½ oz) shiitake mushrooms, finely sliced

½ teaspoon minced garlic

¼ teaspoon minced ginger

pinch of dried chilli flakes

180 g (6½ oz) cooked ramen noodles, prepared as per packet instructions

100 g (3½ oz) silken tofu, diced

1 spring onion (scallion), finely sliced

2 tablespoons toasted pine nuts

LEMON MISO DRESSING

5 teaspoons lemon juice

2 teaspoons white (shiro) miso paste

1 teaspoon tamari

1 teaspoon kecap manis (sweet soy sauce)

1 Pour the sesame and olive oils into a frying pan and warm over medium-high heat. Add the mushrooms, garlic, ginger and chilli flakes. Sauté for 3–4 minutes, until golden brown. Remove from the heat and allow to cool.

2 Toss all the salad ingredients together. Add the mushroom mixture, then tip into your lunchbox.

3 Combine the dressing ingredients in a small jar or container with a tight-fitting lid.

4 Pour the dressing over the salad just before serving and toss well.

CARBONARA RAMEN NOODLE SALAD

Widely adored around the world, carbonara is a classic Roman-style pasta dish combining egg, cheese, cured pork and pepper. This recipe sneaks in some additional ingredients – including peas and chives – and swaps the pasta out for ramen noodles.

2 bacon slices, cut into small dice

180 g (6½ oz) cooked ramen noodles, prepared as per packet instructions

1 hard-boiled egg, finely grated

40 g (¼ cup) peas, blanched

25 g (¼ cup) finely grated parmesan

2 tablespoons finely sliced chives

CREAMY DIJON DRESSING

3 tablespoons creme fraiche

1½ teaspoons white wine vinegar

½ teaspoon dijon mustard

¼ teaspoon minced garlic

salt and pepper, to taste

1 Place the bacon in a non-stick frying pan and cook over high heat for 3–4 minutes, until crispy. Allow to cool.

2 Toss all the salad ingredients together, then tip into your lunchbox.

3 Combine the dressing ingredients in a small jar or container with a tight-fitting lid.

4 Pour the dressing over the salad just before serving and toss well.

HOT 'N' SPICY PRAWN & CHIVE NOODLES

Chilli crisp oil, which forms a large part of the flavouring for this salad, is a chilli-infused oil with crispy bits – such as onion, bell peppers (capsicum), garlic, ginger and peanuts (or soybeans). 'Laoganma' is one of the most popular brands.

180 g (6½ oz) cooked ramen noodles, prepared as per packet instructions

6 cooked prawns (shrimp), peeled and deveined

2 tablespoons snipped chives

1 small spring onion (scallion), finely sliced

handful of cherry tomatoes, halved

small handful of coriander (cilantro) leaves

1½ teaspoons toasted sesame seeds

SWEET SOY CHILLI DRESSING

2 tablespoons chilli crisp oil

2 teaspoons kecap manis (sweet soy sauce)

2 teaspoons water

1½ teaspoons rice vinegar

 Toss all the salad ingredients together, then tip into your lunchbox.

 Combine the dressing ingredients in a small jar or container with a tight-fitting lid.

 Pour the dressing over the salad just before serving and toss well.

CRUNCHY NOODLE
TEX-MEX SALAD

This salad packs in the flavour and has a great crunchy texture thanks to the iceberg lettuce, instant noodles and pumpkin seeds. Toss in some extra jalapeños for an extra-spicy salad.

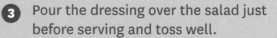

¼ iceberg lettuce, chopped

½ avocado, diced

80 g (⅓ cup) tinned black beans, rinsed and drained

50 g (1¾ oz) feta, crumbled

3–4 tablespoons pickled red onions

2 tablespoons sliced pickled jalapeño chilli

2 tablespoons toasted pumpkin seeds

60 g (2 oz) instant ramen noodles, broken

CREAMY CORIANDER DRESSING

3 tablespoons sour cream or Greek-style yoghurt

1½ tablespoons finely chopped coriander (cilantro)

2 teaspoons lime juice

1 teaspoon olive oil

¼ teaspoon minced garlic (optional)

pepper, to taste

1 Toss the salad ingredients together, then tip into your lunchbox.

2 Combine the dressing ingredients in a small jar or container with a tight-fitting lid.

3 Pour the dressing over the salad just before serving and toss well.

CHICKEN, RAMEN, KALE & ORANGE SALAD

This delicious salad combines noodles, chicken and kale with orange slices and a sweet orange dressing alongside crunchy nuts and seeds. If you like, swap the kale for rocket (arugula) or baby spinach leaves.

180 g (6½ oz) cooked ramen noodles, prepared as per packet instructions

100 g (3½ oz) shredded cooked chicken

handful of finely shredded kale

1 orange, peeled and segmented

small handful of roasted hazelnuts

small handful of pumpkin seeds

ORANGE HONEY GINGER DRESSING

1 tablespoon orange juice

2 teaspoons extra virgin olive oil

1½ teaspoons balsamic vinegar

½ teaspoon honey

1 teaspoon minced ginger

salt and pepper, to taste

 Toss all the salad ingredients together, then tip into your lunchbox.

 Combine the dressing ingredients in a small jar or container with a tight-fitting lid.

 Pour the dressing over the salad just before serving and toss well.

CRAB & SUGAR SNAP PEA RAMEN SALAD

Tinned crab meat is available in various styles,
with varying degrees of quality – so it's always best
to search out good-quality crab meat, to ensure
your salad is the most delicious it can be.

180 g (6½ oz) cooked ramen noodles, prepared as per packet instructions

80 g (2¾ oz) cooked lump crab meat

50 g (1¾ oz) sugar snap peas, blanched

1 small spring onion (scallion), finely sliced

½ carrot, julienned

2 tablespoons snipped chives

small handful of mint leaves

pinch of dried chilli flakes

GINGER SHOYU DRESSING

1 tablespoon olive oil

1 tablespoon rice vinegar

1 teaspoon shoyu (Japanese soy sauce)

1 teaspoon toasted sesame oil

½ teaspoon minced ginger

1 Toss all the salad ingredients together, then tip into your lunchbox.

2 Combine the dressing ingredients in a small jar or container with a tight-fitting lid.

3 Pour the dressing over the salad just before serving and toss well.

SHAVED CABBAGE & PEAR SALAD WITH BACON & CRUNCHY RAMEN

This perfectly crunchy noodle salad combines the classic flavours of blue cheese, pear and bacon. Cut the cabbage and sprouts as thinly as possible – or, if you have a mandoline, shred the vegetables using the thinnest setting.

2 bacon slices, diced

handful of shredded red cabbage

3–4 brussels sprouts, shaved

60 g (2 oz) instant ramen noodles, broken

½ pear, finely sliced

40 g (1½ oz) blue cheese, crumbled

2–3 tablespoons candied pecans, chopped

HONEY MUSTARD VINAIGRETTE

2 tablespoons extra virgin olive oil

1½ tablespoons apple cider vinegar

½ teaspoon dijon mustard

½ teaspoon honey

salt and pepper, to taste

1 Place the bacon in a non-stick frying pan and cook over medium–high heat for 3 minutes, or until crispy. Allow to cool.

2 Toss all the salad ingredients together, then tip into your lunchbox.

3 Combine the dressing ingredients in a small jar or container with a tight-fitting lid.

4 Pour the dressing over the salad just before serving and toss well.

TERIYAKI CHICKEN NOODLE SALAD

Teriyaki is a classic Japanese sauce that can be used with many different types of meats – including beef and pork – but is most commonly associated with chicken. The pineapple in this salad adds a sweetness to the savoury flavours in the dressing.

180 g (6½ oz) cooked ramen noodles, prepared as per packet instructions

100 g (3½ oz) shredded cooked chicken

50 g (⅓ cup) chopped pineapple

1 small spring onion (scallion), finely sliced

1 small carrot, julienned

small handful of shredded red cabbage

2 teaspoons toasted sesame seeds

TERIYAKI SESAME DRESSING

2 teaspoons teriyaki sauce

2 teaspoons sesame oil

2 teaspoons kecap manis (sweet soy sauce)

2 teaspoons rice vinegar

1 teaspoon soy sauce

1. Toss all the salad ingredients together, then tip into your lunchbox.

2. Combine the dressing ingredients in a small jar or container with a tight-fitting lid.

3. Pour the dressing over the salad just before serving and toss well.

KIMCHI RAMEN

This noodle salad takes its inspiration from the flavours of South Korea – with kimchi, wombok cabbage and gochujang paste. There are many different types of kimchi available, so seek out your favourite. Making your own kimchi is also not too difficult.

180 g (6½ oz) cooked ramen noodles, prepared as per packet instructions

50 g (⅓ cup) peas, blanched

3–4 tablespoons chopped kimchi

1 hard-boiled egg, halved

handful of shredded wombok (Chinese cabbage)

small handful of Thai basil leaves (green or purple)

2 teaspoons toasted sesame seeds

GOCHUJANG SESAME DRESSING

1 tablespoon gochujang paste

1 teaspoon rice vinegar

1 teaspoon soy sauce

1 teaspoon kecap manis (sweet soy sauce)

1 teaspoon toasted sesame oil

½ teaspoon water

1 Toss all the salad ingredients together, then tip into your lunchbox.

2 Combine the dressing ingredients in a small jar or container with a tight-fitting lid.

3 Pour the dressing over the salad just before serving and toss well.

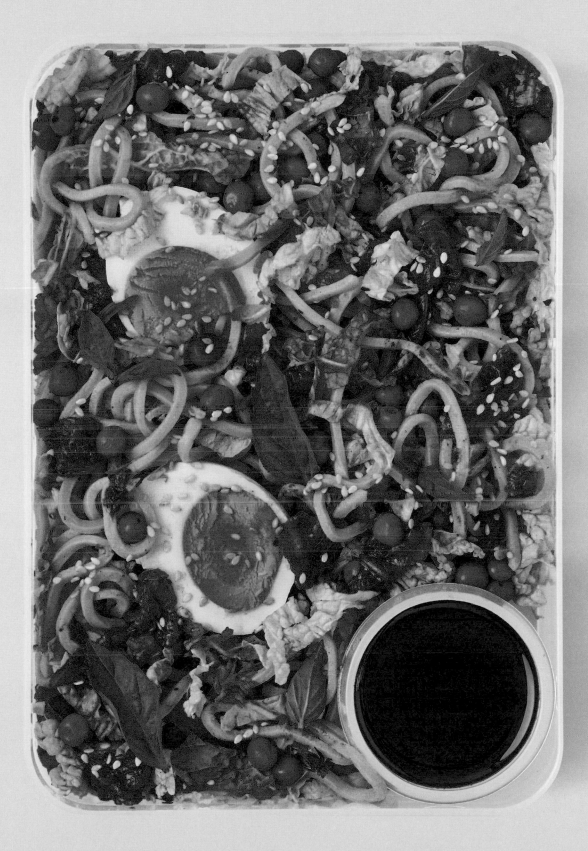

CHICKEN RAMEN WITH CORIANDER & PEANUT PESTO

Pesto is traditionally made with basil leaves and pine nuts and is a popular classic Italian dish. This pesto features coriander and peanuts instead, creating a deliciously moreish Asian-style pesto to flavour the noodles.

180 g (6½ oz) cooked ramen noodles, prepared as per packet instructions

100 g (3½ oz) shredded cooked chicken

½ short cucumber, diced

¼ avocado, flesh diced

small handful of mint leaves

small handful of chilli roasted peanuts

1 lime wedge, to serve

CORIANDER & PEANUT PESTO

30 g (1 cup) coriander (cilantro) leaves

3 tablespoons roasted peanuts

3 tablespoons lime juice

2½ tablespoons sesame oil

1 tablespoon sweet chilli sauce

1 small garlic clove, peeled

1. Place the pesto ingredients in a jug and blitz with a stick blender until well blended. Taste and add a little more lime juice if desired.

2. Place the noodles in a bowl, pour the pesto over and toss to combine.

3. Add the remaining ingredients to the noodles, except the lime wedge. Toss to combine.

4. Tip the noodles into your lunchbox. Add the lime wedge.

5. Squeeze the lime over just before serving.

RICE
NOODLES

THAI BEEF NOODLE SALAD

Thailand is deservedly famous for its iconic beef salad, which is spiked with chilli and herbs, and is much loved the world over. Here we've simplified the dish and tossed it all together with rice noodles.

1 teaspoon olive oil

100 g (3½ oz) minute steak

salt and pepper, to taste

80 g (2¾ oz) dried wide rice noodles, prepared as per packet instructions

½ short cucumber, sliced

¼ red bell pepper (capsicum), sliced

1 small red Asian shallot, finely sliced

handful of mixed Thai basil, coriander (cilantro) and mint leaves

small handful of roasted cashews

SWEET CHILLI GINGER DRESSING

2½ tablespoons sweet chilli sauce

1 teaspoon soy sauce

zest and juice of ½ lime (about 2½ tablespoons juice)

1 teaspoon minced ginger

 Drizzle the oil over the steak and season with salt and pepper. Place in a non-stick frying pan over high heat and cook for 1–2 minutes on each side, until cooked to your liking. Rest for a few minutes, then slice and allow to cool.

 Toss all the salad ingredients together, then tip into your lunchbox.

 Combine the dressing ingredients in a small jar or container with a tight-fitting lid.

Pour the dressing over the salad just before serving and toss well.

DECONSTRUCTED RICE PAPER ROLLS

Fresh (and fried) rice paper rolls are a staple of
Vietnamese cuisine. This noodle dish goes the simpler
route by tossing together all those classic ingredients
into a salad instead – no rolling required.

80 g (2¾ oz) dried rice vermicelli
noodles, prepared as per packet
instructions

100 g (3½ oz) shredded cooked
chicken

2–3 iceberg lettuce leaves,
shredded

½ carrot, shredded

handful of bean sprouts

small handful of coriander
(cilantro) leaves

small handful of Vietnamese
mint leaves

2 tablespoons roasted peanuts

1 lime wedge

LIME CHILLI DRESSING

2 tablespoons sweet chilli sauce

1 tablespoon lime juice

1 teaspoon sesame seed oil

1. Toss the salad ingredients together,
   except the lime wedge, then tip into
   your lunchbox. Add the lime wedge

2. Combine the dressing ingredients in
   a small jar or container with a tight-
   fitting lid.

3. Pour the dressing over the salad just
   before serving and toss well then
   squeeze over the lime.

NUTTY CRUNCHY COLESLAW NOODLES

This salad is a breeze to throw together as it uses store-bought coleslaw, nuts and seeds, alongside rice noodles and mint. The orange-spiked dressing adds a marvellous umami-rich flavour.

100 g (3½ oz) dried flat rice stick or pad Thai noodles, prepared as per packet instructions

100 g (3½ oz) store-bought coleslaw (shredded carrot, red cabbage, white cabbage)

2 tablespoons sugar roasted cashews, chopped

2 teaspoons toasted black sesame seeds

1 tablespoon smoked chilli almonds, chopped

small handful of mint leaves

CREAMY ALMOND MISO DRESSING

2 tablespoons orange juice

1½ tablespoons almond butter

1 tablespoon rice wine vinegar

2 teaspoons white (shiro) miso paste

1 Toss the salad ingredients together, then tip into your lunchbox.

2 Combine the dressing ingredients in a small jar or container with a tight-fitting lid.

3 Pour the dressing over the salad just before serving and toss well.

SASHIMI SEAWEED NOODLE SALAD

This salad relies on getting the very freshest sashimi-grade white fish you can find, and is best made the day the salad is to be eaten. Look for seaweed salads at Japanese grocers or sushi stores.

100 g (3½ oz) sliced white-fish sashimi

100 g (3½ oz) dried wide rice noodles, prepared as per packet instructions

80 g (2¾ oz) seaweed salad (store-bought)

1–2 radishes, finely sliced

1 small green chilli, finely sliced

2 tablespoons wasabi peas, crushed

handful of snow pea (mangetout) sprouts

SOY & PICKLED GINGER DRESSING

2 tablespoons soy sauce

1 tablespoon rice wine vinegar

1 teaspoon sesame oil

1 teaspoon pickled ginger, diced

1 Set the sashimi slices aside.

2 Toss all the remaining salad ingredients together, then tip into your lunchbox. Arrange the sashimi slices on top.

3 Combine the dressing ingredients in a small jar or container with a tight-fitting lid.

4 Pour the dressing over the salad just before serving.

FAT RICE NOODLES WITH SMOKED TOFU, BROCCOLINI & EGG

Smoked tofu is a delicious addition to this noodle salad and doesn't require any preparation – apart from being sliced. Feel free to omit the egg to keep the dish vegan.

80 g (2¾ oz) dried wide rice noodles, prepared as per packet instructions

100 g (3½ oz) smoked tofu, sliced

1 hard-boiled egg, halved

3 broccolini stems, blanched and sliced

40 g (¼ cup) peas, blanched

small handful of bean sprouts

1 teaspoon toasted sesame seeds

CHILLI GARLIC DRESSING

1½ tablespoons soy sauce

1½ tablespoons rice wine vinegar

2 teaspoons chilli crisp oil

½ teaspoon minced garlic

1 Toss the salad ingredients together, then tip into your lunchbox.

2 Combine the dressing ingredients in a small jar or container with a tight-fitting lid.

3 Pour the dressing over the salad just before serving and toss well.

CHICKEN, MANGO & CASHEW NOODLE SALAD

Chicken and mango together are always a winning combination – especially so in this noodle salad. You can replace the bok choy with another leafy green, such as baby spinach, if that's already on hand.

◇◇◇◇◇◇◇◇◇◇

80 g (2¾ oz) dried wide rice noodles, prepared as per packet instructions

100 g (3½ oz) shredded cooked chicken

1 baby bok choy (pak choy), washed well and finely sliced

½ mango, flesh diced

1 small spring onion (scallion), finely sliced

small handful of coriander (cilantro) leaves

small handful of roasted cashews, chopped

TAMARI GINGER DRESSING

4 teaspoons olive oil

1 tablespoon rice vinegar

1 tablespoon tamari

1 teaspoon toasted sesame oil

1 teaspoon minced ginger

1 Toss the salad ingredients together, then tip into your lunchbox.

2 Combine the dressing ingredients in a small jar or container with a tight-fitting lid.

3 Pour the dressing over the salad just before serving and toss well.

FAT RICE NOODLES WITH SMASHED CUCUMBER

This noodle salad is bursting with flavour and a crunchy texture thanks to the cucumber and peanuts. Any size of rice noodle will work with this dish, so use whatever kind you have on hand.

2 tablespoons chopped salted roasted peanuts

200 g (7 oz) short cucumber

100 g (3½ oz) dried wide rice noodles, prepared as per packet instructions

1 tablespoon snipped chives

1 teaspoon toasted black sesame seeds

handful of coriander (cilantro) leaves

CHILLI SOY DRESSING

2 teaspoons tamari or low-salt soy sauce

2 teaspoons toasted sesame oil

2 teaspoons kecap manis (sweet soy sauce)

2 teaspoons rice wine vinegar

1½ teaspoons chilli crisp oil

1. Place the peanuts in a small container.

2. Whisk the dressing ingredients in a bowl until combined.

3. Place the cucumber on a chopping board and use the blunt side of a meat mallet to lightly bash and smash it. Cut in half, then slice into chunks.

4. Toss the cucumber chunks into the dressing, along with the remaining ingredients. Toss again, then tip into your lunchbox.

5. Carry the peanuts separately and sprinkle over the salad just before serving.

PRAWN, PINEAPPLE &
MELON NOODLE SALAD

As fresh as a summer's day, prawns, pineapple, melon, cucumber
and herbs combine in this wonderfully flavourful noodle salad. If
you like things a little spicier, toss in a finely chopped red chilli.

◇◇◇◇◇◇◇◇◇◇◇

80 g (2¾ oz) dried flat rice stick or
pad Thai noodles, prepared as per
packet instructions

6 cooked prawns (shrimp), peeled
and deveined

65 g (⅓ cup) diced pineapple

60 g (⅓ cup) diced honeydew
melon

60 g (⅓ cup) diced short
cucumber

small handful of mint leaves

small handful of coriander
(cilantro) leaves

SHALLOT & GINGER DRESSING

2 tablespoons sweet chilli sauce

1 tablespoon lime juice

2 teaspoons finely chopped
red Asian shallot

½ teaspoon minced ginger

1. Toss the salad ingredients together,
   then tip into your lunchbox.

2. Combine the dressing ingredients in
   a small jar or container with a tight-
   fitting lid.

3. Pour the dressing over the salad just
   before serving and toss well.

DUCK NOODLE SALAD WITH GINGER & HOISIN

This recipe gives a nod to that great Chinese classic, Peking duck. Throw this dish together in peak plum season for the tastiest result.

80 g (2¾ oz) dried rice vermicelli noodles, prepared as per packet instructions

100 g (3½ oz) shredded cooked Chinese duck

3 radicchio leaves, shredded

1 plum, sliced into wedges

1 small spring onion (scallion), sliced

small handful of toasted pecans, roughly chopped

1 tablespoon dried tart cherries

GINGER HOISIN DRESSING

1 tablespoon hoisin sauce

2 teaspoons kecap manis (sweet soy sauce)

2 teaspoons rice wine vinegar

1 teaspoon sesame oil

½ teaspoon minced ginger

 Toss the salad ingredients together, then tip into your lunchbox.

 Combine the dressing ingredients in a small jar or container with a tight-fitting lid.

 Pour the dressing over the salad just before serving and toss well.

SPICY MANGO NOODLES

Sweet and spicy, this noodle salad is a great vegetarian or vegan lunch option for the days you want to go meat free. Bird's eye chillies can pack a punch, so by all means omit it altogether if you're feeling less spicy.

---

80 g (2¾ oz) dried rice vermicelli noodles, prepared as per packet instructions

½ mango, flesh diced

¼ red bell pepper (capsicum), finely sliced

⅛ small red onion, finely sliced

small handful of snow peas (mangetout), finely sliced

small handful of bean sprouts

small handful of mint leaves

1 red bird's eye chilli, finely sliced

3 tablespoons roasted macadamia nuts, chopped

LIME, CHILLI & SESAME DRESSING

1½ tablespoons soy sauce

1½ tablespoons sweet chilli sauce

2 teaspoons lime juice

1 teaspoon toasted sesame oil

1 Toss the salad ingredients together, then tip into your lunchbox.

2 Combine the dressing ingredients in a small jar or container with a tight-fitting lid.

3 Pour the dressing over the salad just before serving and toss well.

SOBA NOODLES

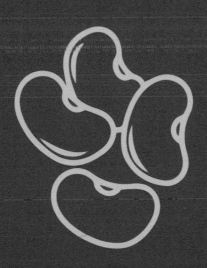

SPRING VEGGIE SOBA NOODLES

~~~

This is the perfect salad choice for those spring months when fresh asparagus is at its best. Go for a good-quality ricotta to really enhance the flavours of this simple salad.

◇◇◇◇◇◇◇◇◇◇◇

180 g (6½ oz) cooked soba noodles, prepared as per packet instructions

4 asparagus spears, blanched and sliced

50 g (⅓ cup) baby peas, blanched

50 g (⅓ cup) broad (fava) beans, blanched

90 g (⅓ cup) ricotta

3 tablespoons grated parmesan

1 tablespoon toasted pine nuts

LEMON VINAIGRETTE

4 teaspoons lemon juice

½ teaspoon grated lemon zest

1 tablespoon extra virgin olive oil

1 Toss the salad ingredients together, then tip into your lunchbox.

2 Combine the dressing ingredients in a small jar or container with a tight-fitting lid.

3 Pour the dressing over the salad just before serving and toss well.

CHILLI CRISP CORN & CHICKEN SOBA NOODLES

Strap yourself in for a real flavour and texture explosion –
corn kernels are cooked in chilli crisp oil and Korean chilli
paste (gochujang) before being tossed through the noodles.
This soba salad promises to be enjoyed on repeat.

1 tablespoon salted butter

1–1½ teaspoons chilli crisp oil

1 teaspoon gochujang paste

100 g (⅔ cup) corn (fresh, frozen or tinned)

salt and pepper, to taste

180 g (6½ oz) cooked soba noodles, prepared as per packet instructions

100 g (3½ oz) shredded cooked chicken

40 g (1½ oz) feta, crumbled

2 tablespoons crispy fried shallots

handful of coriander (cilantro) leaves

SESAME & LIME DRESSING

4 teaspoons lime juice

2 teaspoons toasted sesame oil

½ teaspoon chilli oil

1. Place a frying pan over medium heat. Add the butter, chilli crisp oil, gochujang paste and corn and sauté for about 3 minutes. Season to taste with salt and pepper.

2. Add the drained noodles to a bowl. Toss the chilli corn through, along with the remaining salad ingredients. Tip into your lunchbox.

3. Combine the dressing ingredients in a small jar or container with a tight-fitting lid.

4. Pour the dressing over the salad just before serving and toss well.

SALMORIGLIO SOBA NOODLES WITH TUNA & FENNEL

Salmoriglio is a punchy southern Mediterranean sauce that is most often served with fish. Here, it's tossed through tuna and soba noodles, along with olives, fennel, rocket and capers.

180 g (6½ oz) cooked soba noodles, prepared as per packet instructions

95 g (3¼ oz) tin tuna in olive oil, drained

½ baby fennel bulb, finely sliced, plus some fennel fronds

small handful of pitted green olives

handful of rocket (arugula) leaves

2 teaspoons baby capers

SALMORIGLIO DRESSING

5 teaspoons extra virgin olive oil

1 tablespoon lemon juice

½ teaspoon lemon zest

½ teaspoon chopped parsley

½ teaspoon chopped oregano

½ small garlic clove, minced

1 Toss the salad ingredients together, then tip into your lunchbox.

2 Combine the dressing ingredients in a small jar or container with a tight-fitting lid.

3 Pour the dressing over the salad just before serving and toss well.

TAHINI NOODLES WITH SWEET POTATO, ROCKET & POMEGRANATE

Sweet and bright and tangy, this noodle salad bursts with colour and flavour. Roasted pumpkin (winter squash) can easily be used instead of the sweet potato. To save time, pomegranate seeds can be purchased in packages, rather than having to extract the seeds from the fruit itself.

◇◇◇◇◇◇◇◇◇◇◇

180 g (6½ oz) cooked soba noodles, prepared as per packet instructions

200 g (7 oz) left-over roasted sweet potato, diced

handful of rocket (arugula) leaves

⅛ small red onion, finely sliced

2–3 tablespoons pomegranate seeds

LEMON TAHINI DRESSING

2 tablespoons lemon juice

1½ tablespoons tahini

1 tablespoon water

½ teaspoon maple syrup, honey or agave syrup

salt and pepper, to taste

1. Toss the salad ingredients together, then tip into your lunchbox.

2. Combine the dressing ingredients in a small jar or container with a tight-fitting lid.

3. Pour the dressing over the salad just before serving and toss well.

SALMON SASHIMI SOBA SALAD

With a nod to Japanese cuisine, this soba noodle salad combines silky salmon, creamy avocado, moreish edamame beans and crunchy radishes. Edamame can be found in the frozen vegetable section of larger supermarkets.

◇◇◇◇◇◇◇◇◇◇◇

¼ toasted nori sheet, finely sliced

80 g (2¾ oz) sliced sashimi-grade salmon

180 g (6½ oz) cooked soba noodles, prepared as per packet instructions

toasted sesame oil, for drizzling

50 g (⅓ cup) podded edamame beans (soybeans), blanched

½ avocado, diced

2 radishes, finely sliced

2 teaspoons toasted black sesame seeds

2 teaspoons sliced pickled ginger

PONZU SESAME DRESSING

3½ teaspoons ponzu sauce

1 teaspoon rice wine vinegar

1 teaspoon extra virgin olive oil

1 teaspoon toasted sesame oil

1. Place the nori in a small airtight container. Set the sashimi slices aside.

2. Toss the noodles in a bowl with a little sesame oil. Add the remaining salad ingredients and toss together.

3. Tip the noodle salad into your lunchbox. Arrange the sashimi slices on top.

4. Combine the dressing ingredients in a small jar or container with a tight-fitting lid.

5. Carry the dressing and nori separately. Drizzle and sprinkle over the salad just before serving.

SOBA NOODLES WITH GREEN BEANS, EDAMAME, EGG & DUKKAH

~~~

Dukkah is a popular Middle Eastern spice blend most often made with hazelnuts, sesame seeds, coriander and cumin. You'll often find it in the spice section of supermarkets or specialist retailers – or you can whip up your own blend in no time.

◇◇◇◇◇◇◇◇◇◇◇

180 g (6½ oz) cooked soba noodles, prepared as per packet instructions

10 green beans, blanched

75 g (½ cup) podded edamame beans (soybeans), blanched

1 hard-boiled egg, halved

1 tablespoon dukkah (store-bought)

1 teaspoon black sesame seeds

LEMONY DIJON VINAIGRETTE

zest and juice of ½ lemon

4 teaspoons extra virgin olive oil

½ teaspoon dijon mustard

salt and pepper, to taste

1. Toss the salad ingredients together, then tip into your lunchbox.

2. Combine the dressing ingredients in a small jar or container with a tight-fitting lid.

3. Pour the dressing over the salad just before serving and toss well.

CHICKEN SOBA SALAD WITH ARTICHOKE, SPINACH & GREEN OLIVES

Packed with classic Italian ingredients including marinated artichokes, green olives and parmesan, this sun-drenched salad gives you a taste of 'la dolce vita'. The lemony dressing adds a perfect creaminess.

180 g (6½ oz) cooked soba noodles, prepared as per packet instructions

100 g (3½ oz) shredded cooked chicken

2–3 marinated artichoke hearts, quartered

handful of baby spinach leaves

small handful of pitted Sicilian green olives

small handful of parsley leaves

2 tablespoons finely grated parmesan

CREAMY LEMON & CAPER DRESSING

2 tablespoons mayonnaise

1½ tablespoons lemon juice

1 teaspoon baby capers, chopped

pepper, to taste

1 Toss the salad ingredients together, then tip into your lunchbox.

2 Combine the dressing ingredients in a small jar or container with a tight-fitting lid.

3 Pour the dressing over the salad just before serving and toss well.

GOAT'S CHEESE, LENTIL & BABY BEETROOT SOBA NOODLES

~~~

Pear, goat's cheese and walnuts are a classic French-style combination, often served in a salad along with lettuce. Adding lentils, noodles and beetroot, as we do here, yields a truly hearty lunch.

◇◇◇◇◇◇◇◇◇◇

180 g (6½ oz) cooked soba noodles, prepared as per packet instructions

110 g (½ cup) drained tinned lentils

1 baby beetroot (beet), peeled and finely sliced

½ nashi pear, finely sliced

50 g (1¾ oz) goat's cheese

25 g (¼ cup) toasted walnuts, chopped

SHALLOT & LEMON VINAIGRETTE

5 teaspoons extra virgin olive oil

1 tablespoon lemon juice

2 teaspoons minced red Asian shallot

½ teaspoon dijon mustard

salt and pepper, to taste

1 Toss all the salad ingredients together, then tip into your lunchbox.

2 Combine the dressing ingredients in a small jar or container with a tight-fitting lid.

3 Pour the dressing over the salad just before serving and toss well.

SOBA NOODLES WITH SALMON, CAPERS, SPINACH & DILL

~~~

The horseradish dressing delivers a deliciously spiky punch that makes a perfect foil for the oil-rich hot-smoked salmon. Shichimi togarashi is a Japanese spice blend that lends a little extra spice to this dish – feel free to replace it with cayenne pepper or chilli flakes if you prefer.

◇◇◇◇◇◇◇◇◇◇

180 g (6½ oz) cooked soba noodles, prepared as per packet instructions

80–100 g (2¾–3½ oz) hot smoked salmon, flaked

1 small celery stalk, sliced

1 tablespoon chopped dill

2 teaspoons baby capers

handful of baby spinach leaves

sprinkle of shichimi togarashi

1 lemon wedge

CREAMY HORSERADISH DRESSING

3 tablespoons creme fraiche

2 teaspoons lemon juice

1½ teaspoons horseradish (from a jar)

1 teaspoons baby capers, chopped

salt and pepper, to taste

1 Toss the salad ingredients together, then tip into your lunchbox.

2 Combine the dressing ingredients in a small jar or container with a tight-fitting lid.

3 Pour the dressing over the salad just before serving and toss well.

BROCCOLINI, CHICKEN & HONEY CHILLI SOBA NOODLES

The sweet and spicy gingery dressing gives this salad so much flavour, while the fried shallots and tamari almonds add some real crunch. You can swap the broccolini for shaved cabbage, if you like.

180 g (6½ oz) cooked soba noodles, prepared as per packet instructions

3 broccolini stems, blanched and sliced

100 g (3½ oz) shredded cooked chicken

small handful of coriander (cilantro) leaves

small handful of spiced tamari almonds, chopped

2 tablespoons crispy fried shallots

HONEY, CHILLI & GINGER DRESSING

2 tablespoons chilli crisp oil

1 teaspoon rice vinegar

1 teaspoon honey

1 teaspoon kecap manis (sweet soy sauce)

½ teaspoon minced ginger

1. Toss the salad ingredients together, then tip into your lunchbox.

2. Combine the dressing ingredients in a small jar or container with a tight-fitting lid.

3. Pour the dressing over the salad just before serving and toss well.

GREEN GODDESS SOBA NOODLES WITH MOZZARELLA

Green Goddess dressing is a classic salad condiment that has its origins in 1920s California. It has rightfully remained popular these last 100 years for the deliciously herby and creamy notes it adds to any dish.

180 g (6½ oz) cooked soba noodles, prepared as per packet instructions

1 fresh mozzarella ball, diced

1 spring onion (scallion), finely sliced

2 tablespoons sliced pickled jalapeño

½ short cucumber, sliced

½ small avocado, flesh sliced

small handful of snow pea (mangetout) sprouts

GREEN GODDESS DRESSING

4 tablespoons Greek-style yoghurt

1½ tablespoons finely chopped mixed basil and tarragon

1 tablespoon lemon juice

¼ teaspoon minced garlic

a dash of green sriracha sauce

salt and pepper, to taste

 Toss the salad ingredients together, then tip into your lunchbox.

 Combine the dressing ingredients in a small jar or container with a tight-fitting lid.

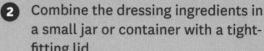 Pour the dressing over the salad just before serving and toss well.

VEGGIE NOODLES

BEETROOT NOODLES WITH ROCKET, ORANGE & CANNELLINI BEANS

~~~~~

To add a little more colour into your salad, swap the purple beetroot for a yellow one when in season, and the orange for a red-tinged blood orange. Toasted pecans or hazelnuts can happily step in for the walnuts.

◇◇◇◇◇◇◇◇◇◇

1 beetroot (beet), spiralised

1 orange, peeled and segmented

100 g (3½ oz) tinned cannellini beans, rinsed and drained

3 tablespoons toasted walnuts, chopped

handful of rocket (arugula) leaves

salt and pepper, to taste

ORANGE & MAPLE DRESSING

1 tablespoon orange juice

2 teaspoons extra virgin olive oil

2 teaspoons apple cider vinegar

1 teaspoon maple syrup

½ teaspoon dijon mustard

1 Toss all the salad ingredients together, then tip into your lunchbox.

2 Combine the dressing ingredients in a small jar or container with a tight-fitting lid.

3 Pour the dressing over the salad just before serving and toss well.

KOHLRABI NOODLES WITH SMOKED TROUT, APPLE & TOASTED PECANS

Kohlrabi – a relative of cabbage, cauliflower and broccoli –
has a sweet, peppery flavour and can be eaten raw or
cooked. It adds a delicious crunch to this trout salad.

150 g (5½ oz) kohlrabi, spiralised

100 g (3½ oz) smoked trout, flaked

1 small apple, cored and finely sliced

25 g (¼ cup) toasted pecans, roughly chopped

25 g (1 oz) dried cranberries

HONEY CIDER DRESSING

2 teaspoons extra virgin olive oil

2 teaspoons apple cider vinegar

1 teaspoon dijon mustard

1 teaspoon honey

salt and pepper, to taste

1 Toss the salad ingredients together, then tip into your lunchbox.

2 Combine the dressing ingredients in a small jar or container with a tight-fitting lid.

3 Pour the dressing over the salad just before serving and toss well.

ANTIPASTO ZOODLE SALAD

A taste of Italy in every bite! For the most delicious antipasto salad, source your ingredients from a good-quality Mediterranean delicatessen.

1 zucchini (courgette), spiralised

4 slices mortadella, roughly torn

5 baby bocconcini

8 pitted green Sicilian olives

4 sun-dried tomatoes, sliced

55 g (⅓ cup) tinned chickpeas, rinsed and drained

1–2 pepperoncini (marinated hot yellow peppers), finely sliced

small handful of basil leaves

HERB & RED WINE VINEGAR DRESSING

1 tablespoon extra virgin olive oil

2 teaspoons red wine vinegar

2 teaspoons minced red onion

¼ teaspoon dried Italian herb mix

pinch of dried chilli flakes

salt and pepper, to taste

1. Toss the salad ingredients together, then tip into your lunchbox.

2. Combine the dressing ingredients in a small jar or container with a tight-fitting lid.

3. Pour the dressing over the salad just before serving and toss well.

ZOODLES WITH CRISP PROSCIUTTO, EGG, ASPARAGUS & MANCHEGO

Manchego is a semi-hard sheep's milk cheese originating
in Spain with a distinct tangy flavour and a crumbly
texture. You'll find manchego in most supermarkets,
but feel free to replace it with a sharp cheddar.

3 prosciutto slices

1 zucchini (courgette), spiralised

5 asparagus spears, blanched and sliced

1 hard-boiled egg, halved

40 g (1½ oz) Manchego cheese, crumbled

1 tablespoon snipped chives

pepper, to taste

CIDER & MUSTARD DRESSING

1 tablespoon extra virgin olive oil

2 teaspoons apple cider vinegar

1 teaspoon dijon mustard

¼ teaspoon minced garlic

1 Fry the prosciutto in a non-stick frying pan over medium heat for about 2 minutes, until crispy, then set aside to cool. (Alternatively, place between two sheets of paper towel and microwave on high for 30 seconds, then remove the paper and allow to cool and crisp.)

2 Toss all the salad ingredients together, then tip into your lunchbox.

3 Combine the dressing ingredients in a small jar or container with a tight-fitting lid.

4 Pour the dressing over the salad just before serving and toss well.

PUMPKIN NOODLES WITH BUTTER BEANS & ROASTED RED PEPPER

To save on preparation time, some supermarkets sell a range of ready spiralised vegetables, including zucchini and pumpkin. The butter beans add a delicious flavour and creamy texture to this salad, but you can easily use cannellini beans instead.

150 g (5½ oz) spiralised pumpkin (winter squash), blanched, refreshed and cooled

100 g (3½ oz) tinned butter (lima) beans, rinsed and drained

1 marinated roasted red bell pepper (capsicum), sliced

⅛ small red onion, finely sliced

45 g (1½ oz) goat's cheese, crumbled

handful of basil leaves

ZESTY LEMON VINAIGRETTE

2½ tablespoons extra virgin olive oil

juice of ½ lemon

½ teaspoon grated lemon zest

¼ teaspoon dijon mustard

salt and pepper, to taste

1. Toss all the salad ingredients together, then tip into your lunchbox.

2. Combine the dressing ingredients in a small jar or container with a tight-fitting lid.

3. Pour the dressing over the salad just before serving and toss well.

CHICKEN 'FATTOUSH' SALAD WITH CUCUMBER NOODLES

Fattoush is a classic Lebanese salad featuring toasted or fried flat bread and zingy sumac. Here we replace the bread with crunchy pre-roasted chickpeas, which you will find in the snack section of most supermarkets.

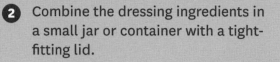

1 short cucumber, sliced into ribbons

100 g (3½ oz) shredded cooked chicken

2 radishes, finely sliced

⅛ small red onion, finely sliced

handful of cherry tomatoes, halved

handful of mixed salad leaves

small handful of mint leaves

small handful of parsley leaves

30 g (¼ cup) roasted chickpeas (store-bought

POMEGRANATE & SUMAC DRESSING

1 tablespoon extra virgin olive oil

2 teaspoons pomegranate molasses

2 teaspoons lemon juice

pinch of ground sumac

1 Toss all the salad ingredients together, then tip into your lunchbox.

2 Combine the dressing ingredients in a small jar or container with a tight-fitting lid.

3 Pour the dressing over the salad just before serving and toss well.

CARROT NOODLES WITH LENTILS & FETA

The purple carrot adds beautiful colour to this salad. If unavailable, use a regular orange carrot instead – or, for a texture and flavour twist, slip in some cucumber ribbons.

1 orange carrot, spiralised

1 purple carrot, spiralised

100 g (3½ oz) drained tinned lentils

50 g (1¾ oz) feta, crumbled

1 small red Asian shallot, finely sliced

handful of mint leaves

small handful of dill leaves

2–3 tablespoons toasted pumpkin seeds

HARISSA YOGHURT DRESSING

3–4 tablespoons Greek-style yoghurt

1 tablespoon orange juice

1 teaspoon harissa paste

1 teaspoon pomegranate molasses

1 Toss all the salad ingredients together, then tip into your lunchbox.

2 Combine the dressing ingredients in a small jar or container with a tight-fitting lid.

3 Pour the dressing over the salad just before serving and toss well.

SALMON & CELERIAC NOODLES WITH A CREAMY DILL DRESSING

Celeriac is a root vegetable that can be eaten raw or cooked. When eaten raw, it has an incredible crunch, with a nutty, celery-like flavour. Here it provides the perfect foil for the hot-smoked salmon.

◇◇◇◇◇◇◇◇◇◇◇◇

150 g (5½ oz) celeriac, spiralised

85 g (3 oz) peppered hot-smoked salmon, flaked

½ short cucumber, sliced

⅛ small red onion, sliced

1 small orange, peeled and segmented

1 teaspoon baby capers

CREAMY DILL DRESSING

3 tablespoons creme fraiche or Greek-style yoghurt

zest and juice of ½ lemon

2 teaspoons chopped dill

salt and pepper, to taste

1 Toss the salad ingredients together, then tip into your lunchbox.

2 Combine the dressing ingredients in a small jar or container with a tight-fitting lid.

3 Pour the dressing over the salad just before serving and toss well.

CUCUMBER NOODLES WITH WATERMELON, OLIVES, FETA & BASIL

This salad takes its inspiration from the classic Greek salad of watermelon, cucumber, olives and feta. A taste of summer, this salad promises to be one to make again and again.

◇◇◇◇◇◇◇◇◇◇◇

1 short cucumber, sliced into ribbons

180 g (6½ oz) diced watermelon

45 g (1½ oz) feta, crumbled

⅛ small red onion, finely sliced

handful of pitted kalamata olives

small handful of basil leaves

small handful of mint leaves

2 tablespoons pomegranate seeds

2 tablespoons chopped or slivered pistachios

POMEGRANATE & SUMAC DRESSING

1 tablespoon extra virgin olive oil

2 teaspoons lemon juice

2 teaspoons pomegranate molasses

pinch of ground sumac

1 Toss all the salad ingredients together, then tip into your lunchbox.

2 Combine the dressing ingredients in a small jar or container with a tight-fitting lid.

3 Pour the dressing over the salad just before serving and toss well.

TUNA NIÇOISE WITH CUCUMBER NOODLES

Tuna niçoise is an iconic French salad that combines salad leaves, green beans, egg, olives, potato and tuna. Here we've switched the potatoes for crunchy radishes and slippery cucumber ribbons. For a spicier salad, use tuna steeped in chilli oil.

1 short cucumber, sliced into ribbons

8–10 green beans, blanched

1 hard-boiled egg, quartered

95 g (3¼ oz) tin tuna in olive oil, drained

2 anchovy fillets in olive oil (optional)

2 radishes, finely sliced

5 cherry tomatoes, halved

⅛ small red onion, finely sliced

handful of mixed baby green salad leaves

small handful of pitted black olives

MUSTARD GARLIC VINAIGRETTE

1 tablespoon extra virgin olive oil

2 teaspoons red wine vinegar

½ teaspoon dijon mustard

¼ teaspoon minced garlic

salt and pepper, to taste

 1 Toss the salad ingredients together, then tip into your lunchbox.

 2 Combine the dressing ingredients in a small jar or container with a tight-fitting lid.

 3 Pour the dressing over the salad just before serving and toss well.

CHICKEN & BASIL PESTO ZOODLES

The pesto dressing is central to the flavour of this chicken and zucchini salad, so search out a good-quality option – or make your own and store it away until ready to use.

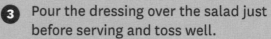

1 zucchini (courgette), spiralised

100 g (3½ oz) shredded cooked chicken

6 baby bocconcini

handful of cherry tomatoes, halved

2–3 tablespoons finely grated parmesan

2 tablespoons toasted pine nuts

small handful of basil leaves

LEMON PESTO DRESSING

3 tablespoons pesto (homemade or store-bought)

1 tablespoon lemon juice

pinch of dried chilli flakes (optional)

1. Toss the salad ingredients together, then tip into your lunchbox.

2. Combine the dressing ingredients in a small jar or container with a tight-fitting lid.

3. Pour the dressing over the salad just before serving and toss well.

INDEX

Smith Street Books

Published in 2024 by Smith Street Books
Naarm (Melbourne) | Australia
smithstreetbooks.com

ISBN: 978-1-9230-4900-0 (hardback edition)
ISBN: 978-1-9227-5499-8 (flexi edition)

Smith Street Books respectfully acknowledges the Wurundjeri
People of the Kulin Nation, who are the Traditional Owners of the
land on which we work, and we pay our respects to their Elders
past and present.

Publisher: Paul McNally
Editor: Katri Hilden
Series designer: Kate Barraclough
Photographer: Jacinta Moore
Food stylist: Deborah Kaloper
Printed & bound in China by C&C Offset Printing Co., Ltd.

Book 304
10 9 8 7 6 5 4 3 2 1

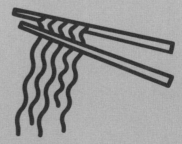